Dropshipping for Heroes

Andres Zamriver and Loly Zamriver

Published by Andres Zamriver, 2021.

DROPSHIPPING FOR HEROES

First edition. July 9, 2021.

ISBN: 979-8201046118

Written by Andres Zamriver and Loly Zamriver.

We dedicate this book to all the haters, and to the people that will read it but won't take action hence you are the motivation for those of us who DO! oh and to the neighboors that kept on having epic parties and forcing us to stay up all night.. so we kept busy and wrote this book, enjoy!

Dropshipping for Heroes

How to Get Your Dropship Business Up and Running Quickly and Profitably

Table of Contents

Introduction

Online retail is blowing up. There are no two ways about it. In fact, online retail in the United States is expected to hit $638 billion in annual value by the year 2022.

According to some estimates, there are millions of e-commerce pages, e-commerce businesses and dedicated websites on the internet. That's how big e-commerce is.

Online retail has completely changed consumer buying behavior. In turn, consumer behavior has changed online retail. This is a mutually reinforcing process. As more and more people buy mobile devices like tablets and smart phones, e-commerce opportunities continue to rise.

Think about it, previously, if you only accessed the internet through your laptop or your desktop at home or at the office, there is less space for impulse buys. Maybe you're driving in your car and you think about something that you needed to buy or would like to buy. At that point, you'd have to wait until you can get in front of a computer to possible research your prospective purchase. Not anymore.

If you are driving and you're with somebody, you can say, "I have an idea. Why don't we buy this?" And then whoever is with you can look it up on his or her mobile phone or tablet.

This is how a lot of people buy stuff. It doesn't matter whether you're looking for products or services, the mobile revolution has really exploded online purchases. This is an industry that continues to grow by leaps and bounds. We haven't seen the peak yet.

If you need proof of this, you just have to look up the fact that more and more malls in the United States are being bulldozed or converted into other types of structures. That's how profound online retail has become.

People are not shy to buy online. In fact, in many cases, they expect to buy online. It's more convenient. They can buy whenever they want, they can buy based on their terms, and most importantly, they can compare different products as well as different retailers before making their final decision.

In previous decades, this was simply impossible. Unless you had all the time in the world and a tank full of gas, it didn't make much sense for you to do a lot of price comparison or to hop from shop to shop asking a lot of questions. Thanks to the internet, you can do that all within minutes and you don't even have to leave the comfort and convenience of your living room, or your car for that matter.

Given these reasons, it is no surprise that more and more people are setting up shop on the internet. More and more entrepreneurs such as yourself are putting up their own online store. In fact, there are millions of online sellers.

Whether you are selling strictly on EBay or you have your own dedicated website, there is no shortage of entrepreneurs trying their hand at online commerce. Think about it, that's a huge pie to slice up. $600 billion plus is a lot of money.

Unfortunately, it's not all sunshine and rainbows as far as online retailers are concerned. A high percentage of them do not make any money. In fact, many of them go out of business.

According to many sources, in excess of 90% of all startups and companies on the internet fail within the first four months. Imagine that, 90%.

We're not just talking about simple blogs here. We're not just talking about online publishers looking to make a few bucks here and there when people click on ads. We're not just talking about affiliate marketers either. These are people who make money when visitors enter their email address on forms on their websites. These also include online retailers.

Again, it doesn't really matter whether you are operating out of EBay completely or you have your own dedicated online store. Your rate of success doesn't depend on whether you have a warehouse and a full retail infrastructure or you just have a storefront.

The sad reality is that this 90% failure rate is avoidable. This is especially true when it comes to online retailing.

How come? Well, first of all, online retailing can be a logistical nightmare. If you are going to set up your own standalone online retail shop, you have to do a lot of things.

First of all, you have to get inventory. You also have to set up shipping properly. Also, you have to reach out to manufacturers and ensure a steady supply chain.

If you own your own online store with your own brand, you are solely responsible for labeling and packaging. This includes graphics design.

Also, you have to make sure that all your merchandise is stored safely in the right warehouse. You have to pay rent on that warehouse. You have to also pay insurance.

Not only that, when people place an order for whatever it is you are selling, you have to make sure that the right products get picked up and put in the right envelopes.

Now, if you think the previous process is a headache, wait, there's more. In the event that a customer is not happy with what they receive, you would have to make sure that you have a customer service infrastructure set up. These are people who would respond to emails or actual phone calls.

Whether you have an actual call center in the United States, Canada, Western Europe or Australia, or you outsource this to outfits based in India or the Philippines, you have to have such an infrastructure in place. Every single month you have to pay to keep that infrastructure intact.

If you think all of this quite a handful, this doesn't even include marketing and promotions. Make no mistake, there are a lot of pieces that have to fall into place for your online retailing dream to turn into an actual real world business empire. Online retailing is no joke.

The worst part to all of this, if all these processes are not bad enough, is that a lot of your expenses are upfront. You have to pay for your initial inventory, you have to set up your infrastructure, and you have to have enough cash to burn for at least six months until your sales can catch up.

The problem here is that you only make money when you move stock. That's right, you make money only when you sell.

It is no surprise that a lot of people who try to set up an online retail business the traditional way ends up failing. They find out in the worst way possible that online commerce can be expensive, slow, time consuming, and at the end of a day, yield a very low return on investment.

In fact, a lot of the people who set up online stores ten years ago have gone out of business because they found out that they were pushing low margin products. We're not talking about small companies here. Look up toys.

It was a venture-funded company that had millions of dollars in backing. It went belly up very quickly. It turned out that spending $10 dollars on shipping a $2 bag of dog food did not make much financial sense.

Thankfully, a lot has changed since the wild popularity of e-commerce ventures in the 2000's. There is now an alternate model. This alternative requires less capital up front.

In fact, in many cases, the only capital you have to spend goes to your website or your store builder and some pieces of software. That's pretty much it. Everything else is going to be funded by your actual sales.

This alternative e-commerce business model enables you to run a leaner and faster organization. You only pay for your inventory when you get a sale. Compare this to buying tons of stuff without any clear assurances that they will actually sell. It doesn't even compare.

Also, refunds and customer support can be automated and dealt with very quickly. In fact, in many cases, a lot of entrepreneurs who use this alternative model don't even bother with hassling their customers regarding the merchandise.

They don't bother to check if the item was really broken, defective or whatnot. Instead, they just require the customer to ship the merchandise to be returned and they will automatically refund or exchange the item. No questions asked.

How are they able to do this? Well, in many cases, their profit margin per item is so high that they can afford a significant percentage of their sales ending up in refunds or returns. You can't say the same about traditional online retailing. It doesn't even compare.

What's the name of this alternative online store business model? Dropshipping.

In this book, I'm going to step you through the process of setting up a dropshipping business and promoting it so you can start turning a profit quickly.

I understand that there are many other dropship books out there. But unfortunately, they're heavy on the hype and light on the actual information you need to succeed.

This book is different. I focus on what's important. I step you through the process and give you enough information so you can get going quickly and take the right steps to increase your chances of success.

Other books hype you up on dropshipping. I'm telling you, it doesn't matter how excited you are, if you're doing the wrong things, you're going to produce the wrong results. It doesn't get any simpler than that. This book is the antidote to all of that.

Chapter 1

Drop What? The Working Definition of Dropshipping

When people first hear the word dropshipping, all sorts of mental images come to mind. The most common, of course, is some sort of package at the end of a parachute being dropped from the sky. Others think about somebody making millions of dollars hanging out at the beach playing around with his computer. Well, the reality is somewhere in between.

Dropshipping is a business model, but ultimately, it is a fulfillment model. It is a way of filling orders. Instead of you setting up your independent standalone e-commerce infrastructure, you leverage the fulfillment capabilities of your supplier.

Here are the key components of dropshipping.

Your Supplier Does Most of the Fulfilling

When you get an order through your online store, your software will automatically purchase the item from your supplier. This triggers a lot of processes that you would have been responsible for if you had set up a standalone, traditional e-commerce store.

What will your supplier do for you? First, your supplier will have your products in stock. These are the products that you are advertising on your website. Set up properly, your automated or semi-automated dropshipping system ensures that whatever items you advertise on your store will be available at your source.

Next, your supplier will take care of the warehousing. They're doing this already since they're selling merchandise to many other customers besides yourself. Instead of you renting out your own warehouse and paying a monthly lease as well as insurance for it, you just leverage the warehousing infrastructure your supplier has.

Your supplier also picks out the product. This is a big deal. Generally speaking, if you are going to be running your own standalone traditional online store, you would have to have somebody in a back room somewhere going through products, picking out items that a customer has bought. This is very expensive because you have to pay that person in terms of wages and mandatory benefits. You also have to pay insurance for the premises just in case somebody gets hurt.

Don't think that when you hire somebody in the United States or in most parts of the world that your labor costs begin and end with the wages of your staff. There's a lot more additional costs that may seem invisible to you, but these are costs nonetheless.

After your supplier's personnel has picked out the product your customer ordered, they will label it. Again, you save a lot of money here because you don't have to worry about being responsible for this yourself.

The product is then packaged and shipped out to your customer. This is the key with dropshipping. When a buyer orders from your store, you turn around and order from another store. But instead of having the product shipped to you, it gets sent to your customer.

In the event that your customer needs a refund or file some sort of complaint, you handle that. The dropshippers doesn't handle this. You can resolve this with your supplier later on. But when the refund request or complaint comes in, you have to handle these.

The good news is that most dropshippers sell products that have such a fat margin that they just request the customer to send them back the item. If the customer has enough time or remains motivated enough to send the item, the dropshippers then issues the refund or replacement.

Since your profit margin is big enough, you don't have to hassle with verifying if an item was actually broken or if it was mislabeled. Just to take care of the issue, you have a "no questions asked" refund policy.

Believe it or not, when you require your customer to ship or repackage the item they're complaining about by a certain deadline, this usually takes care of the problem.

How come? Most people are busy. Most people either forget or they just don't have the time. In the big scheme of things, it's really not going to be worth their time and bother to send back an item that costs around $20.

Of course, different people have different thresholds. For some people, $20 is a lot of money and it's definitely worth their time and attention. For other people, 20 bucks is nothing. Regardless, by simply asking that your customers send you back the merchandise, you pretty much cut down on refund and complaint issues.

The good news here is that dropshipping margins are often high enough that you will be able to absorb a certain percentage of your sales ending up in returns or refunds.

Chapter 2

The Benefits of Dropshipping

In the previous chapter, I covered the definition of dropshipping. Once you have compared this fulfillment model with the traditional fulfillment model for e-commerce, the benefits should be pretty much clear to you.

But just in case you're still wondering if this is the right model for you, I'm going to lay out the specific benefits you will get. All of this, of course, impacts your bottom line.

At the end of the day, it all boils down to profit or loss. You want to pick a model that is more likely to help you generate a profit.

Most people don't go into business to lose money. The only entity I can think of that eagerly goes into ventures with the understanding that it might lose money is the government. But other than that, most people want to turn a profit.

This is why it's really important to wrap your mind around the key identifiable strategic advantages of dropshipping. I'm confident that once you have gone through all these benefits, you would quickly realize that this is probably the model for you.

I used the word "probably" because you might have personal business connections that might ensure or increase the likelihood of success with the traditional model. Unfortunately, most people are not in that position, so it is my understanding that most people would choose dropshipping because of the following benefits.

Low Startup Costs

Just how low are we talking about? Well, since you don't have to pay for your stock ahead of time, and any purchase you make will be covered by your actual customer, dropshipping has very low upfront costs. You only need to put up a website.

This, of course, can be broken down into other costs. You need to pay for hosting and a domain name. You also have to make sure that your website looks attractive enough so people would want to buy from it.

Also, you would need certain software to make sure that when people go to your website to buy something, you don't have to actually work to process that order. You have to buy software that will automatically buy from your source. This way, you don't have to babysit your online store.

Even after you've spent money on all of these, the total that you would have spent would still be a fraction compared to a warehouse lease, a container truck full of initial products, labeling equipment, insurance, wages for staff, and on and on it goes. There is no comparison.

Your initial costs for a dropshipping business is a drop in the bucket compared to what your costs would have been if you were to set up a traditional online store.

Process-Driven Ordering

You only pay for your stock when you get an order. Compare this with buying inventory ahead of time, storing it in your warehouse and hoping against hope that somehow, some way, somebody would buy something. It doesn't even compare.

When somebody shows up at your online store to buy a product that you're advertising, your software turns around and orders that product from the source. That's the only time you pay for your stock. You don't pay ahead of time.

You Get to Cherry Pick Products From Different Sources

Another great thing about dropshipping is that you are able to feature products from many different sources on your online store. Now, you can do this too with a traditional e-commerce store, but it's going to be very costly.

Why? You're going to have to stock all the items that you are putting up for sale on your online store. This means that you're going to store all these products at your warehouse. They take up a lot of space and they increase your warehouse space needs which, of course, leads to you paying a higher lease.

You don't have to worry about that headache with dropshipping. On its face, it looks like you have everything all in one place. The customer doesn't know that when they order different products, you are actually ordering from many different places.

Your Supplier Mails Orders Directly to Your Customer

This is one of the biggest advantages of dropshipping. Instead of you charging your customer for shipping or having to pay it out of pocket, your supplier mails the product directly to your customer.

Please understand that there's a lot more going on here than just the shipping. The supplier has to pick out the right product from their inventory. They have to label it or package it, then they have to ship it. Each step of the way costs time and money.

With dropshipping, all these costs are shouldered by your supplier. You don't have to worry about any of that. The only thing that you have to worry about is receiving payment from your customer paying your supplier and taking care of whatever returns, refunds or complaints you get. That's all you have to worry about.

Supplier Ordering can be Easily Automated

If you were to do dropshipping manually, you'd go crazy. Seriously. It's a lot of work.

When orders come in, you have to take the order form, and then transfer all that information over to the order form of your supplier. All sorts of mistakes could be made. This takes a lot of time and labor.

Thankfully, dropshipping can easily be automated. There are specialized pieces of software available on the market that takes customer order information from your website and transmits it to the order form of your suppliers.

The best part to all of this is that you don't have to be there to actively monitor the transmission of this data. You can be sleeping, you can be taking care of your kids, you can be on a vacation on the other side of the planet, it doesn't matter. You don't have to be physically in front of a computer to make sure that each and every order is processed correctly. It can be automated based on the rules that you have set up.

This is the reason why a lot of people make great passive income with dropshipping. They just set up the store once, and maybe work a few hours every week, and the store pretty much takes care of itself. At the end of the week or the month or whatever reporting period you select, you get payments.

Your payments are pretty straightforward. It is what's left over after you have received money from your customers and paid your suppliers for the products you purchased. This is your gross revenue.

Online Store Builder Tools Automate Everything Including Payment Processing

Please understand that there are two payments going on with dropshipping. In the previous sections I talked about the payment that you have to make when you turn around and order whatever it is your customer bought from your online store. This is crucial because you're not going to have a stock to pass on to your customer if you don't pay your supplier.

However, you have to make sure you take payment on your own website. This is called "payment processing."

Traditionally, online stores used merchant accounts and other traditional processing methods that were a headache. Thankfully, things have advanced to the point that you can set up your store with an online store builder that automates your websites handling of payments.

When people whip out their credit cards and enter their card info on your form, everything is handled and processed by the software you installed. This software is engineered into the store builder that help you put up your store in the first place.

This was not the case as recently as ten years ago. Back then, you basically had to build everything from scratch. You had to build a website separately from the payment processing, and then you had to layer on other technology.

Not anymore. There are standalone packages that you just need to install on your WordPress site and customize. In fact, a lot of these store builders are so sophisticated and powerful yet easy to use that you only need a few keystrokes and mouse clicks to put up a professional looking online store.

Remember the Secret Sauce

As awesome as dropshipping's benefits may be, and they are quite amazing, please understand that there are a lot of people who are doing the same things you're doing. You have to choose a strategy that would make your online store stand out. This is the key to success in dropshipping.

If I were to tell you that all you needed to do was just set up a generic dropship site, find generic products on the internet from suppliers and set up the right software, I would be misleading you. Seriously. I would only be giving you part of the story.

What makes all of this come together is branding. If you don't have a private label, which is your brand, what you have, really, is a commodity.

The author of the personal success classic Rich Dad Poor Dad, Robert Kiyosaki, said, "If you don't have a brand, you have a commodity." I want you to wrap your mind around that quote. This is the secret to your success in dropshipping.

Why? Well, when you sell commodities, ultimately, the only thing you can compete on is price. A commodity, by definition, is a product that has no distinguishing features from other products of its type on the market.

When farmers produce corn all over the United States, that corn is indistinguishable from other corn produced in other farms. In fact, that corn is indistinguishable from corn produced in Canada, Mexico, China, or elsewhere. The only thing distinguishing commodity items from each other is, of course, the price.

This is exactly the place you don't want to go. Why? When you compete based on price, you're going to be engaged in a race to the bottom. Seriously.

You think you can produce corn at a very low price? Think again. Maybe in China the weather is really great and there's enough water that they come up with a bumper crop.

What do you think the effect would be on your end of the market? Of course, there will be downward pressure. This is why globally; a lot of farmers struggle because of price fluctuations. This can all be traced to the fact that they are cranking out commodities.

When you adopt a private label strategy for your dropship business, you take yourself out of the commodity game. You create a brand.

You have to understand that McDonald's, regardless of what you think about its quality, is a brand. When people look for burgers, they will pay a premium for the McDonald's brand.

The same applies to Starbucks. When people look for coffee and they insist on Starbucks, it goes without saying that they are willing to pay a few bucks extra for the Starbucks brand.

Everybody knows that if you just wanted a nice, hot cup of coffee, you can get it for a much lower price. But that's not what you're looking for. You're not looking for commodity coffee. You're looking for the Starbucks brand.

That's how powerful brands are because they help you get out of the dead end of commodity merchandising. This is the first secret that I need you to thoroughly understand. I want this to be crystal clear in your mind. You have to have a brand.

Again, if you don't have a brand, you have a commodity. Commodity selling is usually a losing proposition. You'd have to move a tremendous amount of products to generate a decent profit. That's how commodities work. They operate on volume.

With brands, you might have essentially the same commodity, but people are willing to pay a premium. How about that? That's where you want to be.

The Second Secret

Now that I have you excited about private labeling, you probably are feeling a little bit apprehensive. After all, your experience with brands probably involve Louis Vuitton, Gucci, Chanel, Nike, and Apple Computers.

You're probably thinking that if you set up a brand, which is your private label, it's going to be expensive. Believe it or not, labels don't have to be expensive. Seriously. This is the second secret. You have to have a graphic that people can easily recognize.

Coming up with that graphic and having it printed out and slapped on whatever product that you're selling doesn't have to be expensive. A lot of would-be dropshippers are under the impression that the moment they start thinking about branding and getting private labels, then their overall expenses just explode. No, this is not true.

You have to understand that all you're doing is selling what would otherwise be a generic no-name product and slapping a label on it. That mere act elevates the perceived value of your product.

What if I told you that a lot of the electronics in your home are actually indistinguishable from no-name, no-brand electronics? The only difference, of course, is the Samsung, LG or Sony label. I know it's crazy, but it's true.

This is called original equipment manufacturing or OEM. Whether we're talking about mobile devices, computers or cars, OEM is the rule. However, your perceived value varies tremendously depending on the label that's slapped on that car, computer or mobile device. Do you see how this works?

You can play the same game. It doesn't have to be expensive, but you can make so much more money, thanks to the increased perceived value of the products you are selling.

DROPSHIPPING MODEL

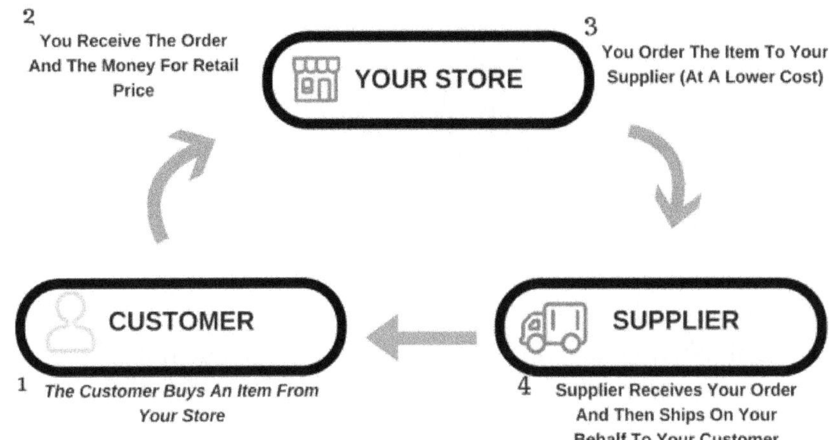

To Brand or Not to Brand

At this point, you're probably all excited about private labeling. At this point, you're probably thinking that this is the way to go because you get such a massive competitive advantage. Well, here's the thing. To some people, this is not a clear cut, black and white decision.

When you are selecting between selling a brand or going with a no-brand item, you have to balance what you stand to gain with what you have to give up. When you sell a no-brand item, you get to sell quicker and cheaper. People are already buying that no-brand item, so basically, you're just going to sell faster because you lowered the price.

Now, that may work for some time, but eventually, somebody will undercut you. You may be thinking that you are dominating your market right now, but what if somebody found another supplier with the same exact quality and product features? This means that you're going to have to lower your price, and then they lower their price, and on and on it goes.

But you do get to hit the market faster and cheaper. After all, you're not spending extra on branding. You're not getting a brand specially designed and labels printed, and you're not getting those labels put on your product.

If you go with the branded approach, you would have to pay your supplier to put your label on the items they are shipping for you. This is always a risk. Why? The products may not sell.

You can fetch a higher price for them, but you'll only benefit from this if they sell in the first place. Do you see how this works? You have to think about the pros and cons.

I suggest that you go with the no-brand approach first, learn the ropes, and figure out the game on a volume basis. After you have established a reputation for yourself, give that reputation a home in the form of a brand. That's when you would have enough cash to work out a deal with your suppliers.

If you play your cards right, these processes will flow into each other and you will end up coming out ahead. Let's put it this way, you're more likely to end up in a much better place than if you just stuck with the generic product approach.

In the next chapter, I'm going to lay out a winning dropshipping blueprint.

Chapter 3

Your Winning Dropshipping Blueprint

Make no mistake there are tons of dropshipping guides and blueprints out there. I'm not going to lie. This blueprint that I'm going to share with you is probably not the first you have come across. However, I am convinced that it should be the last that you should read because it's the only one I know that actually works.

If you want to be a **Dropshipping Hero**, this is it. Seriously. All the other dropshipping guides and online courses that I have a checked out in the past and researched simply falls short. That is the long and short of it. They either miss a very important section or they are so focused on getting you excited about becoming a dropshippers.

Why would they want to do that given there is a 90% failure rate in all online businesses? Well, they want you to get so excited that you sign up for a course after course after course. They want you to buy one product after another and, at the end of the day, they leave you holding an empty bag.

If you're sick and tired of that kind of experience you have come to the right place. You are reading the right book because the following dropshipping blueprint is going to make you a dropshipping hero.

You just have to follow every step and make sure they fit your set of circumstance. As long as you follow the directions and you tweak certain sections to fit your circumstances and experiences, you will be fine.

Here is my winning dropshipping blueprint.

Pick a niche

•Filter your niche based on market factors

•Pick a product or create a master list of products you'd like to sell

•Pick a supplier or suppliers

•Get a private label deal

•Get a label designed or get brand graphics custom designed

•Send your design files to pour supplier

•Get some samples manufactured and shipped to you

•Put up your brand-labeled store using a store builder with your brand graphics on your store

•Set up your payment processing and dropship backend software

Scheduling

Please pay close attention to this. This is crucial. Please understand that the blueprint is going to break down the different steps you to take to set up your successful dropship business.

However, please note that a lot of these overlap so once you have started on one part of the blueprint, it's probably a good idea to start on other parts that overlap with it. This way you're not wasting a lot of time waiting for one process to start and stop and then switching to the next process. A lot of these can be pursued simultaneously.

The key here is not to wait because since there are so many things to do, you probably will end up delaying the launch and promotions of your dropship store by several months if you were to do these sequentially.

The Master Schedule

Here's the master schedule in terms of sequencing.

FIRST STAGE

Niche Research and Product Research

•Niche research

•Filter niche based on market factors

•Vendor research at AliExpress

•Final product selection

These are items that you should do first.

SECOND STAGE

Brand Design

•Identify a brand persona

•Get a brand graphic design

•Decide on the final graphic

THIRD STAGE

Store Building

•Get a domain

•Get hosting

•Install WordPress

•Set up WooCommerce

•Set up your payment processing system

•Set up AliDropship[1]

•Incorporate your brand graphics into your website

•Brand Product Labeling (Since this is in the same stage as store building, you can do this at the same time you're building your store)

•Send graphics to supplier

•Get branded products packaged bay supplier

Shortcut

---

1. https://alidropship.com/?via=3773

Use AliExpress Agent to buy your products and relabel them. They will dropship for you. They also will help with pictures and directly source deals for you from China.

FOURTH STAGE

Store Launch

- Test or Soft Launch - This is not the full official launch of your website.
- Full official launch

Promotions

- Press release
- Quora campaign
- Social media marketing campaign
- Social media curated content publishing campaign

Mailing List

Build your mailing list and start sending update e-mails.

Chapter 4

Niche and Product Research

Let's get one thing clear. If you build your dropship store around the wrong niche, you probably will fail. It's that simple. You have to pick a niche that is growing. You cannot just pick up a random niche that you think may sell may be hot. You can't just trust your gut instincts on this.

Unless you have had many years of experience dropshipping successfully, you shouldn't follow hunches. You have to do your research.

First, you have to look at what's selling on eBay. eBay is one of the largest e-commerce platforms on the planet. Pay attention to what's hot on eBay.

One way to do this is to click through every category on eBay and you will see a list of products. Pay attention to the categories that have a lot of products with the word "hot" right next to them. If you come across a category that has mostly hot selling products, you are in a hot category. You're in a niche that enjoys a tremendous amount of demand.

Once you have a short list of popular categories, go on over to Amazon to cross-reference what you found. On Amazon, you can search for Amazon product categories. Search for the same types of products that were labeled hot on eBay. These are products that appear in what seems to be very popular eBay categories. Take a look at the sales rank of those products on Amazon. The lower the number, the better.

Line up all the categories that you've researched and identify the category that has the most top-selling Amazon items in it in terms of sales score. If you did your homework right, you should have identified the right niche.

Now, this leaves out a very important detail. Niches can be very big.

For example, home audio recording electronics. You have to then pick a winning product in your niche. This is not as easy as you think. You have to understand that, generally speaking, the lower the price of an item, the more units you can sell.

However, there's a limit to that. If it's too cheap, people might think that you're selling low-quality stuff. So, you have to shoot for something in the middle. Look for the retail price range of specific products you're thinking of selling. See if they sell for a nice little range by looking them up on different e-commerce sites on the Internet. Don't just focus on Amazon. Look them up on eBay as well.

Once you have found lots of products in hot niches or product categories that have a decent price range, you're going to do one more level of analysis. Think about the target market for that product.

Will people be needing this product once and then maybe buy after a very long time? Are they going to be buying it once but they will be back in a fairly short time? Finally, do you think they would continue to buy this item?

Usually, when items come at a low-enough price point, consumers can start looking at that item as disposable or a recurring purchase. Disposable razors are the first thing to come to mind. Or razor cartridges.

Keep this in mind. There is a correlation between the price and how often people would need that item.

Also, if you are sure that people would only buy that item once in a very long time, this tells you that you should look for an item that sells for a fairly high price on average.

Select Your Product

By this point, you should have shortened your list of niches and products, and you're ready to pick a specific type of item to sell. Please understand that if you want to succeed in this game, you have to sell a brand. As I mentioned earlier in this book, if you don't have a brand, you have a commodity.

Commodity selling is a tough business. It's a volume business. It's going to be very hard for your little online dropshipping store to drive that kind of volume. This is why you need to focus on selling that on the kinds of products that would be easy for you to brand.

There are two ways you can do this. You can look at the product that you're thinking of selling and see if it's brandable or if it's rare enough.

If it's rare enough, you may get away with not branding it. You may be able to get away without getting your custom-designed brand added to the dropship product and having it put in special packaging. You can dispense with all of that if the product is rare enough. What do I mean by this? Well, look for that specific product on Amazon and eBay as well as Shopify.

Also, do random searches for online stores selling that product using Google. If it turns out that there are relatively few resellers selling that product, you may be able to get away without having it branded. However, if there are a lot of people in your niche selling basically the same product, you're going to be in trouble if you don't slap a brand on that product.

Next, start thinking about pricing. A lot of online entrepreneurs and would-be online store millionaires are very excited at this point. They think this is where the magic happens. If only things were that simple.

You have to understand that when you mark up your product, it has to be within an acceptable price range within your niche. If you followed the instructions above correctly, this not to be a problem.

The marked-up price of your product must be within an acceptable range. This means that it shouldn't be too cheap or too expensive. It has to be within a decent range because remember you're not competing on price so there's no need to shoot for the low end of the price range. Your main selling point is not price. Your main selling point is your brand.

However, you shouldn't use that as an excuse to charge an arm and a leg. That's no good either because the more you charge, the higher equality and service expectations of your customers. Also, the less orders you would get because demand is affected by price.

You might get stuck with a double whammy. You might end up putting yourself in a position where it takes a long time for you to sell a product and when you do, it almost gets automatically refunded because your target customers are very discriminating have very, very high expectations.

Shoot for something in the middle.

Further Product Research

I wish I could tell you that by this point, you should stop. I wish I could tell you by this point, you should have enough of a hunch as to what will work and what won't work. No, that's not going to work.

Why? You need to base your decisions on numbers. Why? There has to be some sort of objective basis why you pick one product over another. This is crucial.

In the analytical steps above, you've already taken care of parts of the picture but there are other pieces that you need to deal with.

First, look for actual search demand for your type of product. This is very important. At this point, you've already looked for your type of product so you know the keywords that people use to find that type of product.

Go to Google AdWords and use their keyboard planner tool. Enter your product's keywords into this tool. You should be able to see the monthly average search volume range of the type of products you're thinking of selling.

Stay away from products that have very, very low search volume. Similarly, stay away from products that have a very high search volume. Chances are there's going to be a lot of competition for those. Again, shoot for something in the middle.

Next, look up the CPC value of those keywords. CPC stands cost per click. This is the amount of money advertisers would pay Google to show ads related to those keywords. This should give you a rough idea of the commercial value of your product.

It also gives you an idea of how competitive your product space is. Obviously, when competitors outdid each other to get the top spot, this shows that there's a lot of competition. Worse yet, this competition has deep pockets.

Filter Your Niche Products Based on Market Factors

By this point, you should still have a fairly decent list of products that you're investigating. Again, you should have started with a niche list and then a huge product list. By this point, that list is getting shorter.

You should also have related keywords to your product. Enter those keywords into Google's search box one by one. Pay attention to the number of websites that sell your product. This should give you a rough idea of how much competition there is for that type of product. Remove from your list products that have just simply too much competition.

Next, enter your keywords into Google Trends. Pay attention to the search volume trend. Do you see it going up over time or do you see a flat line? Worse yet, do you see a line that's curving down?

You know you're looking at the right product when you see a nice upward search trend for it. Now, don't look for anything spectacular. Don't look for a trend line that is like a 45-degree going up.

Even a nice little gentle slope up is good as long as the timeline is long enough. Regardless of what you do, stay away from products that are trending downwards or that have flat lined. There's a good change that once search trends for a particular type of product flat lines that it's only a matter of time until it starts to dip down.

You need to do this analysis because you don't want to sell a product that will eventually fall out of favor. If you need a good example of this, look up fidget spinners. They were all the rage a few years ago. Now, people have forgotten about them and moved on.

You don't want to put up a dropship site that specializes in this product because the demand will dry up sooner or later. Maybe it will have a nice little revival after a few years but before then, you probably would be using losing money on the maintenance costs of your website. No matter how you look at it, the ROI might not be there. So, focus on a product that is enjoying an upward trend line.

Finally, look for competitors for your product. These are people who sell basically the same type of product. They may have different brands but it won't matter. Look for the product functionality and features. What's the price difference between them? This should tell you everything you need to know about how much you should charge for your own product.

Make sure you compare apples to apples. Look at all the features they bring to the table and then compare them based on the features they have. It doesn't make sense for you to compare the price of a product that has five features to another product that only has two features. So, make sure you do roughly equivalent comparison in terms of features before looking at pricing.

At the end of this stage, you should have a clear idea on what product to sell. In fact, you may even have a short list of products you are thinking of dropshipping.

In the next chapter, I'll step you through the process of finding a supplier using AliExpress. Why AliExpress? AliExpress already has Chinese manufacturers and distributors who are willing to dropship. They know the game. It's not like they would sell in very small quantities like one item, but they will ship it to your customer.

This is a modified version of Alibaba. The problem with Alibaba is they offer much lower prices straight out of China; however, you need to buy a whole container load. Also, you have to get a line of credit or prepay for the stuff.

AliExpress is the dropshipper's dream come true because you're dealing with Chinese manufactures and distributors who are willing to sell in single-item lots. That's a big deal because usually when you deal with a wholesaler, they will give you a break on the price provided you order in bulk. Not exactly dropshipping friendly.

AliExpress is the way to go because you deal with sources straight out of China and they have very, very low pricing. I'm continuously amazed at just how cheap stuff can be on AliExpress.

See you in Chapter 5.

Chapter 5

Product Selection

At this point, you should have a fairly decent list of products you're thinking of selling. These products have been filtered through the steps I have described in the previous chapter. You're probably excited about these products because they're trending well. They sell at a good price and they obviously have decent demand levels. What's not to love? Well, there's one problem. You have to find a supplier.

This is where AliExpress comes in. As I mentioned in a previous chapter, AliExpress is great because they sell items in small lots. They're not like Alibaba that requires huge volume purchases paid for in advance or through a line of credit that you have to physically ship from point A to Point B. AliExpress deals with many AliExpress vendors and deal in single quantities. They do the shipping for you. Many of them also will private label for you.

But please understand that private labeling is an extra. This is something that you have to ask for. It's a good idea to follow the steps below and then take the extra step of contacting the vendor to ask for private label options. First, you need to go to AliExpress and look for the category most associated with the products you're thinking of selling. Look for your product there. If it's not there, look for the product type. At this point, you should filter your list.

Your list should start to shrink quickly because a lot of products that you're thinking of selling may not currently be available on AliExpress. Next, filter suppliers based on their price. Now at this point, you should have found vendors for the product you're trying to sell. The next step is to filter them by price. If the price they're charging is too high, then that's no good.

Take that vendor off your list. Look for vendors that sell at a low enough price so that when you add your profit margin you are in the middle of the price curve you have researched previously. If you did your homework and followed all the previous steps, you know what that price curve looks like. You want to be right in the middle. When you factor in how much each particular vendor is charging for the product, you should have a clear idea of what your product margin will be.

In this situation, look for the cheapest seller that can deliver roughly the same quality as other vendors. This way carves out a healthy profit margin. I can't emphasize this enough because your profit margin must be so healthy that even if a significant percentage of your sales and in-returns or customer complaints, you still make a nice profit.

Obviously, if your profit margin is like 10 percent, this is just not going to happen. Not even 50 percent. Thankfully with AliExpress, there are many product categories where the profit margins of over 100 percent are possible. So look for those. At this point, your list should be getting really short.

Next, look at shipping, they must ship for free. This is non-negotiable. The shipping must be free because if you ask the buyer to pay for shipping, this will change the total price of the products you are selling. And it may well turn out that your offers are not that competitive. Finally, look for a vendor that has a decent shipping turnaround time. They have to be quick enough.

Some vendors simply don't care. They will ship your stuff when it gets there. Meaning it can take close to a month or two months. That's simply not acceptable considering the fact that more and more online shoppers are being conditioned by retailers like Amazon to demand two days, three days, or at most one-week shipping. If your online store's turnaround time is so radically different from your competitors, then your visitors probably won't buy.

Shortcut #1 Using a WordPress Plugin Called AliDropship[2]

You can access AliExpress and search within AliExpress using this plugin. The best part of this plugin is that you will be able to auto-import products that you've selected to sell to your store. Once you make a selection, AliDropship will automatically import the selected items into your online store's database.

---

2. **https://alidropship.com/?via=3773**

3

This, of course, requires that you have your website up and have installed WooCommerce which is your online store builder. Still, AliDropship[4] is a great shortcut because you don't have to manually go through AliExpress. You can apply a wide range of filters. Another great thing about the AliDropship plugin[5] is that it updates automatically.

As you probably already know as a shopper that sometimes when you go to Amazon Seller, they run out of the items you wanted to buy. This happens. But with AliDropship[6] when you select a product to sell

3. https://alidropship.com/?via=3773
4. https://alidropship.com/?via=3773
5. https://alidropship.com/?via=3773

on your website, the software automatically synchronizes availability between your website and the vendor you're sourcing the product from. This auto-updating system ensures that you have the latest info from your vendor.

So if they run out, your buyers will see that there is no item available. This way you don't end up selling an item that you cannot fulfill because your vendor doesn't have any. Another great feature of this plugin is pricing automation. Keeping track of pricing is not a problem if you are only selling a handful of items in your online store. But if you're selling dozens or even hundreds of items, it can easily turn into a headache.

The great thing about AliDropship[7] is when you select products to sell and they import their information, the software automatically adjusts the pricing of these products based on preset profit margins that you have specified. You just set up the rules and your supplier's products will be repriced on your website. The best part of this feature is that you can do it for only a few specific products or all the products on your site. This way you can set different profit margins for different products. Pretty neat.

AliDropship's[8] Bread and Butter

The main reason why people buy the AliDropship plugin[9] is that it fulfills your orders automatically. You don't have to do anything manually. When somebody places an order on your online store, it goes straight to AliExpress, orders the necessary items, and fulfills the product. You can be sleeping. You can be enjoying the day out at the beach with your family or you can be reading a book. There's no need to babysit your online store because AliDropship does it all for you.

---

6. https://alidropship.com/?via=3773

7. https://alidropship.com/?via=3773

8. https://alidropship.com/?via=3773

9. https://alidropship.com/?via=3773

Powerful Shipping Filtering Technology

As I mentioned above, you want to pick a vendor that will ship in a fairly quick period of time. One way to do this is to filter vendors that support e-packet shipping. This is a free shipping option and it's very fast. Unfortunately, if you were to go through AliExpress listings manually, it's going to be very hard to try to spot these. You might even miss a really good vendor because you're trying to finish things quickly. AliDropship[10] does it for you.

Basically, you can set it as a filter. They will only list vendors that have that feature. Finally, many online stores don't have order tracking. When you go to these stores and you buy something, you're pretty much on your own in terms of figuring out how your orders coming along. With the AliDropship plugin[11], the software checks the open orders that you have.

It then looks for tracking updates and communicates these via e-mail to your customers. This actually makes you look good because customers that are made aware of the status of their order are less likely to complain. You'll also build customer loyalty here because it's obvious that you're not taking them for granted or forgetting them. Instead of doing this manually, you can do this using software and this can mean a big difference in terms of building a brand.

Read This If You Want Private Labeling

When you filter your vendors, make sure you also follow this step if you want to sell branded products. You have to use AliDropship[12] or any other plugin tool to filter out vendors. Once you have a nice list of vendors, take this extra step. Get in touch with them regarding labeling.

You might have to set up a custom deal with them where they would have your stickers and whatnot ready so they can apply your

---

10. https://alidropship.com/?via=3773

11. https://alidropship.com/?via=3773

12. https://alidropship.com/?via=3773

brand to items you buy. Of course, this means that you're going to have to pay more per item unit. This also requires you sending them packaging and label materials ahead of time.

Please note that not all suppliers will accommodate this because this is an extra step on their part. But this is why you have to make sure you get a good deal with them to make it worth their while. In other words, they will charge you more for each unit than they normally charge a low price for. The extra mile, of course, covers the extra time and effort they take to ship out your stuff.

Generally speaking, if you have proven yourself to a vendor by ordering a huge amount of products in a fairly short period of time, you would not have a problem with private labeling. In fact, if your order volume is so high, they might even do this for absolutely free. In other words, they're not going to change the base price of the items you are reselling from them. But you've got to reach that stage first. And oftentimes, this means cutting a special deal.

Shortcut #2 Use AliExpress Agent

The great thing about AliExpress agent is that they are a dropship option specifically geared towards private label sellers. They have set up their operation in China to buy products for you and they will handle everything else. They will handle labeling. They will dropship for you. They will also take great photos of the product. This way you have everything you need to sell a branded product on your website.

The downside to AliExpress agent is that they charge extra for their services and you also have to prepay for your inventory. This is going to be a deal killer for many dropshippers who are just starting out. However, if you notice that you can pretty much sell a specific type of product from a vendor at a very predictable rate, you might want to hire AliExpress agent. Of course, you should only do this if your manufacturer or distributor doesn't want to private label stuff for you.

Still, having a dropship partner with operations out of China helps tremendously. Especially, I'm excited about their photo services. This is a big deal because if you want to market on social media like Instagram, Pinterest, Facebook groups, or Facebook pages, you need a lot of graphics. The more graphics, the better. Of course, this can be solved fairly easily if you just buy an item directly from your vendor and they send it to you and you take pictures.

But maybe you don't have the skills to do this or the manpower to do this or maybe just too much of a hassle. Also, this is going to be a big problem if you are trying to photograph a huge product line. Even if you have the skills and the time to take photographs, it might just be too much of a hassle if you have an extensive product line that's just on offer at your store. AliExpress agent is an option. I suggest that you revisit this once you've gotten quite big and you're ready to do private labeling.

Now, please note that usually vendors, suppliers, and manufacturers would only private label if your volume is really high. You might find yourself in a kind of like a middle ground position where you're not selling at such a low volume that your only option is regular dropshipping with no labels. However, you're not selling enough to get a special deal with your manufacturer or distributor. If you're in that middle ground, an AliExpress agent makes a lot of sense.

However, once you reach a really high sales volume level, I would strongly suggest that you work directly with the manufacturer to get them to absorb the cost of private labeling your stuff. This is a win-win situation because you have developed a solid-enough brand that gets a lot of sales and they are selling a lot because of you.

So the incentives are definitely there at that point. As I mentioned, if you're just starting out, you probably don't have much choice in the matter and just need to go with regular non-branded dropshipping until things peak up and you can then scale up.

Chapter 6

Brand design and other important graphics

It's easy to dismiss designing a brand as a purely graphics design project. I'll bet you right now that if you ask any person that's just passing by you as you read this how they define a brand, they will either mention McDonald's, Starbucks or some other graphic symbol. They're not completely wrong, but they're not completely right either.

Please understand that your brand is more than the logo you pick for your business. Your brand is something more. Successful businesses understand this. They don't focus on coming up with a memorable-looking graphic. That goes without saying. You must do that anyway. What is more important is your selection of the values that you communicate with your brand.

Remember that you still have a brand even though you're not showing people your logo. Even if people have no idea what your logo looks like, they can still appreciate your brand. In fact, the moment anybody mentions the name of your business, they should be able to zero in on your brand. That's why your brand goes beyond graphical representations. It's more than your logo.

What is a brand?

Simply put, your brand is the association people have between certain values and the experience or results your business brings to the table. Pretty heavy stuff, right? You probably think of things this way. Well, this is the difference between brands that you will remember for a long, long time and brands that you interact with every day and just as quickly forget.

There is a difference between people actively looking for McDonald's regardless of where they are on the planet and the logo of a corner burger store. Sure, if you're visiting your local area, you probably would head to that corner burger shop. But that's pretty much the extent of your brand loyalty. On the other hand, if you like McDonald's food and you find yourself in Eastern Europe, South Africa, the Middle East or Japan, you probably would head to McDonald's.

Why? There are certain values being communicated by the McDonald's brand. Again, this goes beyond the graphics. What values do people associate with McDonald's? They associate a certain dependable level of quality. That is to say, they are assured that regardless of which McDonald's branch they eat at, whether it's in Manila or Mumbai or Munich, chicken nuggets will still have the taste, texture and aroma of chicken nuggets from a McDonald's branch in New York City.

They are also expecting a certain level of friendliness, openness and cleanliness. This indicates a sense of belonging, a sense of hospitality. These are the values that people associate with the name McDonald's.

That's why McDonald's is a global brand. The same applies to Starbucks with a slightly different set of values. Do you see what's going on here?

A brand is simply a set of values you want your customers to associate with the service or merchandise your company provides. At the end of the day, you are providing an experience. You're not just selling stuff that you drop ship from some place in China. This goes beyond that. Because if you want to make it in this game, you have to develop a brand.

As I mentioned at the beginning of this book, if you don't have a brand, you have a commodity. People will basically look at the stuff that you're selling as a mere starting point in their shopping journey. They'll basically just say, "Thank you for the idea, but I'm not going to buy from you. I'll buy from somebody else." That's how commodity buyers think.

There is no compelling reason for them to buy from you instead of somebody else who offers the exact same thing as you. When you build a brand, those values that people automatically associate with your business are worth dollars. They can mean the difference between buying a no-name product of the exact same quality and buying your product at a 300% markup.

That's how it works. That's how the game is played. Until and unless you build a brand, you're playing this drop shipping game to lose. It's only a matter of time until a competitor undercuts you or your supplier screws up and you switch from supplier to supplier. This leads to all sorts of disruptions and you may not be able to compete with other stores offering the exact same stuff.

Understand the power of branding. How do they do this?

Begin with reverse engineering

The first thing that you need to do is understand your niche. For example, you're selling bug zappers. Look for your competitors. How do they brand themselves? What do they focus on? Usually, in this industry, the main focus is on safety and convenience. Bug zappers can make for more comfortable summer nights. Who wants the hassle with all those bug bites?

Also, there is a strong element of health security. In certain parts of the United States, there are all sorts of mosquito-borne diseases. In addition to these are service-related values. Look through your competitors' brands. Pay attention to what they highlight. You should be able to see a pattern. Start with those. Then look for specific values that would distinguish your business from theirs.

Maybe you should focus on being your customer's friendly neighbor. Maybe you should focus on dependability and ease of access. Think in terms of values. Think of how you can continue to repeat the appeals to these values until your potential customers associate your brand with these values. That's how you get ahead. You can't just show your logo over and over again and say, "This is my company."

People would say, "So what? I see logos all the time. What makes your company different?" That's where you have to step up. The answer to that question must be the loudest part of your messaging.

Come up with a branded domain

Once you've studied your competitors, you might want to seriously consider buying a branded domain. Instead of bugzappers.com, buy a domain based on your brand name. This way, nobody can steal your thunder. They can't register bugzapper.net, .org, .biz, .mobi or anything else. More importantly, the more you expose your brand and communicate it to the greater world, the stronger the association people with have between your brand and certain experiences they desire or values they hold dear.

Register your domain name

The next step in your blueprint is domain registration. You can use a wide range of registrars. A registrar is simply a registration service that takes your name and assigns a domain name server address to it. The registrar then takes all queries from browsers requesting your domain name and points them to the server where your website actually is.

Believe it or not, your unique identity is located on the server where your data is. The problem is, that unique name is a number. It's very hard for people to remember a long string of numbers. They can, however, remember Google.com, Yahoo.com and Amazon.com. We think and remember in terms of names. You can register your domain name with NameSilo.com or GoDaddy.com.

Personally, I would go with NameSilo.com because privacy registration is already included in the low fee you pay. With GoDaddy, you have to pay separately for the domain registration and privacy. Regardless of which registrar you go with, make sure you include the DNS number your hosting company gives you.

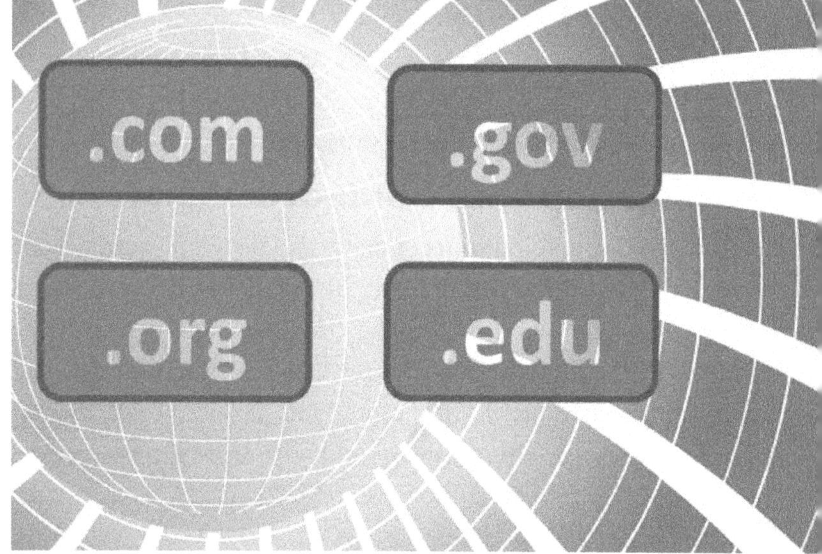

Sign up for a hosting service

A hosting service is a company that rents out space on computer hardware. The hard drives or storage resources of these computers house your information. The service providers, in turn, are connected to the backbone of the internet or a big data pipeline. You need hosting because without hosting, nobody is going to see your store.

Your website is really just a bunch of 1's and 0's on a hard drive or storage device somewhere. Your hosting company ensures that when users request your domain name, this request is routed to their domain name server, which then routes the browser to the computer that has your information on it. Hosting ensures that you are found on the internet.

It's very important to find and sign up for a hosting company that is known for uptime guarantees. In other words, they will ensure that your website is pretty much round the clock. This is a big deal. If your website goes down from time to time, you may be losing money hand over fist.

It really would be quite sad for you to put in all this time, effort and energy, drumming up traffic only for visitors to draw a blank when they go to your site. Make sure you host your website with the right company. Well-known hosting companies include Bluehost and DigitalOcean or LiquidWeb.

Install WordPress

Most hosting packages have some sort of administrator panel included in their service. You just need to log into the administrator panel and you can see all sorts of functions for your hosting account. Again, you are renting either a complete computer or a portion of that computer. When you log into an administration panel, you can set up email, as well as set up WordPress.

With a few mouse clicks and keystrokes, you can easily set up WordPress on your hosting account. It's pretty straightforward. You just need to click the Install WordPress feature and make sure you associate it with the domain name you bought for your online store. Everything else pretty much involves you just filling out a form.

Once you have reverse engineered your competitors' brand graphics and you have a clear idea of what values you want your brand to be associated with, the next step is to get some design work going. You can go to places like Fiverr where designers will produce a logo for you for as little as $5. The downside to Fiverr is the fact that the less you pay, the spottier the quality.

I'm not saying that all the logo designs you will get for $5 are going to be substandard. I'm not claiming that. What I'm saying is that you have a higher chance of getting low-quality work than if you paid a higher price for premium graphics on Fiverr. Fiverr used to only charge $5 across the board. Now, service providers can charge a wide range of prices.

Generally speaking, the higher the price you pay, the more options you get. Maybe you get more revisions. Maybe you get more creative work or some other special benefit. Whatever the case may be, review the past work of each graphic designer and communicate with them very clearly what you're trying to achieve with your brand graphics. They must be on the same page as you.

If you are looking for a more consistent quality to a more consistent talent pool for your brand graphics, you might want to consider hosting a contest at 99designs. 99designs is a website that attracts graphic artists from all over the world who compete in design contests. This includes logo, header and other types of web graphic designs.

The minimum price you can offer is $200. The great thing about 99designs is that you get a lot of participants, especially if you pay a higher bounty, and you get to choose among participants' outputs. This increases the chances you would attract highly professional and skilled logo designers who can capture the values you want associated with your graphic brand.

Brand product labeling

Once you have approved a final version of your graphic brand, make sure you ask for an original PSD file version of it. This is extremely important. PSD is the Photoshop file for your graphic. You need that PSD file because you're going to send it to your supplier. Your supplier should be able to resize or otherwise scale your graphic when printing out your specialty packaging or labels.

This is how you get branded products. Your supplier would print out your brand graphics in the form of a sticker or write on the packaging itself.

Shortcut

If you don't want the hassle with your supplier about specialty packaging because you don't know if they would do a good job, use aliexpressagent.com. They will relabel your products and they will also buy your products for you. Then they will drop ship to your customers. They also help with pictures and they are quite handy sourcing direct deals from China.

Now, if you're just starting out, I would not suggest aliexpressagent.com because it can get quite pricey. Also, you're going to have to buy a certain amount of products from them so they can apply your brand packaging on your inventory. This kind of defeats the purpose of drop shipping. The whole point with drop shipping is that you are not paying upfront. You only buy from your supplier when you receive an order.

However, if you are selling branded items, aliexpressagent.com is a good midway solution. You may not have the volume that would justify cutting a special deal for private labeling with your vendor, but you want to do something more than just offering unbranded products.

APPROVED

Chapter 7

Building your store

By this point you already have a domain and you already have a hosting account. I also already talked about using a direct administration panel to install WordPress. In this chapter, we're going to talk about building your store using your WordPress installation. If you were to do this on your own from scratch, you're going to have to be some sort of tech genius because it's going to be quite time and labor intensive coming up with your own specialty design store.

It's doable if you have the skill set, but it's going to take quite some time. A lot of people simply do not want the hassle with a website designed from scratch. This is where WordPress really shines. A lot of people are under the impression that WordPress is just a blogging platform. Sure, originally, WordPress enabled bloggers to put up websites very quickly and create unique-looking sites thanks to its skin system.

Bloggers can also enjoy a wide range of functionality on their blogs, thanks to WordPress' plugin system. You just have to install a plugin to get new functionality for your WordPress site. Maybe you want a message board. Maybe you want to play videos. Maybe you want a specialized database. All these and many other functionalities are possible through the WordPress plugin architecture.

WordPress is that versatile and flexible. In fact, WordPress is so flexible that you would be surprised as to how divergent the look and feel of many WordPress-based sites can be. Some website may look like an auction site, but it's actually based on WordPress. It can look like a typical blog. It can look like a job search platform or a classified ads website. It can even look like a news aggregation site.

This is how robust the WordPress platform is. Accordingly, you should use the tremendous database power WordPress brings to the table. How? Pay attention to the following.

Install WooCommerce plugin

I highly suggest that you use the WooCommerce plugin. If you want to build a store quickly, just get WooCommerce. It is a free plugin that enables you to build online stores. You can design your store and stock products using the WordPress platform. It also offers automatic tax calculations and inventory management.

Think of WooCommerce as a platform you install on WordPress. When you install WooCommerce, you can create different types of stores depending on the specific designs you select. Also, it is a technology platform because you can use extensions that will help you process payments and make your content more social media friendly. You can even plug it into Fulfillment by Amazon. You can also use extensions to track shipping, as well as interact with your mailing list using services like MailChimp.

What makes WooCommerce different from Shopify and other hosted store builders?

The difference between WooCommerce and Shopify, besides the fact that the main platform is free, involves the ownership of your data. When you use WooCommerce, you will be installing it on a server you control. It's going to be on your domain name, which is tied to your hosting service. In other words, you control your data. You can download your data, back it up and move it.

This is not the case with Shopify. With Shopify, you are building your online store on their platform, which they host themselves. The big advantage of Shopify is that you don't have to worry about updates or security issues. Since you are using a hosted service, all that security work is done centrally by Shopify.

On the other hand, since you have your own hosting running WordPress and WooCommerce, you're going to have to make sure that your server is fully updated and you have adopted core security functions. What makes WooCommerce stand out is the fact that it encourages developers to produce plugins or extensions for its platform.

It uses an open-source architecture, and this enables developers to come up with a wide range of extensions. There are, of course, official and unofficial extensions. In terms of the actual count of official extensions, there are more than 400 existing. These can help you create an affiliate program, manage your database better, make your content more presentable, make your content more viral, and so on and so forth.

Another great thing about WooCommerce is that it's just like WordPress in that it used a theme-based platform. Meaning, there are tons of themes you can use to change the look and feel of your WooCommerce-based store. Maybe if you change your product line, you can easily swap out your theme to reflect the change in your inventory.

In fact, this environment is so open-ended that you can pretty much customize the complete look and feel of your store. If you get the right help to modify your themes, the only real limit to the appearance of your store is your imagination and creativity.

Finally, since WooCommerce is built on the WordPress platform, there is built-in blogging support. You can publish a lot of content to promote your products. This is a big deal because unless you're going to be spending a lot of money on paid traffic, it helps to create content that bolsters your brand instead of using a standalone service for this. There is no need for this because WooCommerce is built on a WordPress foundation.

You can use AliDropship plugin to find a proven and high-converting theme for your store, it's easy to do it yourself.

Other features WooCommerce brings to the table

You can embed your products. You can activate payment processing. Buyers can check out from any page on your website. WooCommerce also has a robust categorization, tagging and product attribute system. This makes it easier for your customers to find a wide range of products you stock. You can also turn on product ratings and customer reviews. This is social proof and goes a long way in encouraging visitors to buy from your store.

AliDropship[13] Setup

Once you have installed the AliDropship plugin[14], just go to the official AliDropship[15] site to look for themes that you can install right

13. **https://alidropship.com/PLUGIN/?via=3773**

away. The most High-Converting Themes can be found on AliDropship.com/themes[16]. Its most popular free theme is Storefront and Michelangelo. You can start there. This theme can easily be modified. You can also try other paid themes available in AliDropship[17]. You would have to pay for these because they are geared towards specific types of products.

One of my favorite stores is in the gaming niche and I used a free AliDropship Theme[18], take a look at my final result: https://gamingbaseman.com

Regardless, one you have installed AliDropship, you only need to go to AliDropship.com[19] and look for available extensions that will not only help you change the look and feel of your store, but you can also include payment processing, shipping tracking, email list integration and even affiliate marketing. There are just so many directions you can go with AliDropship.

It is no surprise that it's one of the most recognized names in online store building. The best part is you are fully in control because it is a local installation on your server. You're not renting space from a company that is in control of your data. It's important at this stage to make sure that you plug in your brand graphics. This is pretty straightforward.

The themes that you get or buy through AliDropship[20] will prompt you as to where to put your brand graphics. Depending on the theme you get, you may have to get your graphics resized. This is usually not a problem if you have the source copy or PSD of your graphic files.

---

14. https://alidropship.com/PLUGIN/?via=3773
15. https://alidropship.com/PLUGIN/?via=3773
16. https://alidropship.com/themes/?via=3773
17. https://alidropship.com/themes/?via=3773
18. https://alidropship.com/themes/?via=3773
19. https://alidropship.com/?via=3773
20. https://alidropship.com/PLUGIN/?via=3773

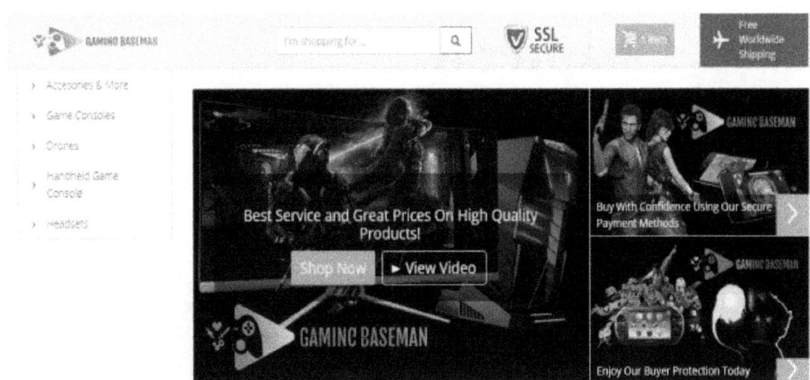

SUPER SALE UP TO 80% OFF ALL ITEMS! LIMITED TIME OFFER

Chapter 8
Product Data Importation

After you have installed AliDropship[21] and the high-converting theme for your store, the next step is to setup the plugin correctly. Once you've uploaded this to your server, you need to configure it with the AliExpress products you have decided to sell. Whip out your research notes regarding the products from AliExpress that you are interested in selling.

Using the AliDropship plugin, filter those products based on the ePacket feature and other filters. Once you have identified the merchant that you want to buy from, import product details into your database. AliDropship makes this so easy. With just a click of a button, you get information directly from AliExpress. Most importantly, AliDropship would now synchronize your listing of that product with whatever updated information is available at AliExpress.

---

21. https://alidropship.com/PLUGIN/?via=3773

This way, if your vendor runs out of the product you're selling, the available quantity shown on your website will be set to 0. This is a big deal because drop shippers can easily get into hot water when they process the payment of a buyer and then turn around to find out that there is 0 availability of their source. You end up stuck. Worse yet, the clock is ticking. For every passing day, your customer can get more worried and upset.

This constant update from AliDropship takes care of that headache. Once you have imported your product details into your database, make sure that you make changes to this information. Maybe you imported too much information and you'd want to strip it down or you did not get enough. Whatever the case may be, do not settle for whatever information you automatically imported from AliExpress.

Get good photos

Get clear, crisp, high resolution product photos. If you are selling branded merchandise, make sure your photos really highlight your logo or your brand. The key is to make your products look as appealing as possible. The rule of thumb I follow is pretty straightforward: the larger the pictures, the better. Insist on very big pictures.

This is not always possible if you're just getting pictures off AliExpress. Once you have sold the product a few times, get in touch with the merchant and see if they can give you better pictures.

Do not neglect your product descriptions

It's extremely important to make sure that you have product descriptions that people would want to read and be influenced by. These are two closely related things, but they are different. Unfortunately, a lot of drop shippers are content to just copy and paste the product description their supplier uses. This is going to be a problem. It really will be. Why? Your competitors are doing the exact same thing.

Don't assume that just because your visitor checked out your store, that means that this person did not check out other stores similar to yours. If you are just simply showing the same product description for your merchandise as in AliExpress, your prospective customer is probably going to just focus on price. In the back of their minds, they're thinking, "Since you're just offering the same stuff as everybody else that I've checked out, let me see your pricing."

Again, this is not a good position to be in. You shouldn't compete based on price. This is why I suggest that you put a lot of time, effort and energy in writing product descriptions that sell. Please understand that there is a big difference between a product description that describes merchandise clearly and one that sells. These are two totally different things.

In fact, this is so sensitive that you might want to get professional help. Services like Ozki.org specialize in mission-critical, high-value product description. Their product descriptions try to create an emotional connection between the prospective customer and your brand's values.

If you have very little money, you might want to get product descriptions from places like Fiverr. However, as the old saying goes, you get what you pay for. Please remember that your product description is not just a piece of text. It is what will make or break your business. If you cannot convert the visitor on the product description page, you probably won't convert them at all. You lost that sale.

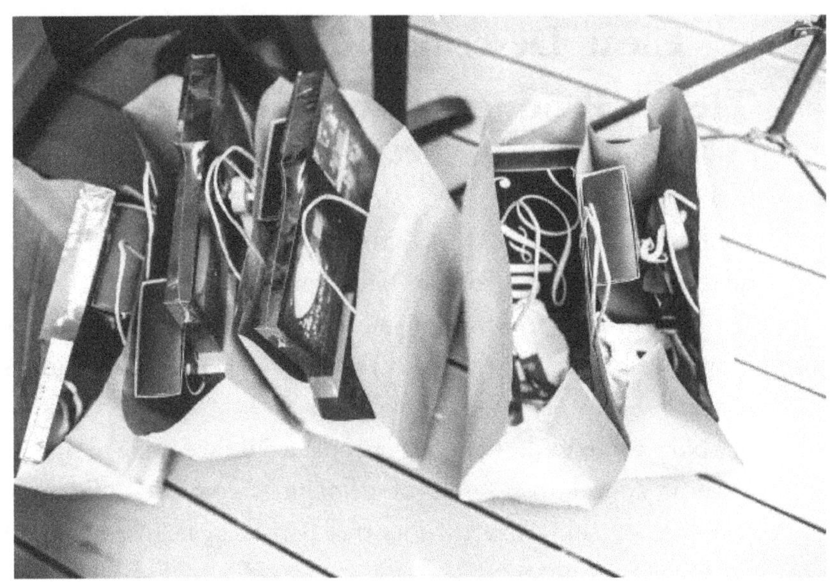

5 Key Hallmarks of Effective Product Descriptions

Again, I can't repeat this enough. Your product descriptions will make or break your online store. Do not screw this up. Next to niche product selection, this is the most important part. If you do not feature descriptions worth reading, you are going to fail. It doesn't get any simpler than that.

Sooner or later, you will fail. Why? At best, your business what continue to struggle by making cents on the dollar; at worst, you're not going to convert any of your visitors at all. That's how crucial your product descriptions are.

There are five key hallmarks of effective productive descriptions. You need to get all these right. This is why I suggest you get in touch with professional product description writers from places like ozki.org, Upwork, or Fiverr.

Hallmark #1

Clear Description of Personal Benefits Tied to Product Features

Let's get one thing clear. When people buy products, they're not looking to buy products per se. Instead, they're looking to buy benefits. Understand how that works. They're looking to answer that classic question "What's in it for me?" with your product.

Your product description must answer that in very clear terms. How? Well, look at the product that you're selling. What features does it have?

Now try to understand why people would see value in that feature. Does it appeal to a sense of belonging, comfort, safety, security, convenience? How exactly does that particular feature bring value to the life of your buyer?

Even if you're selling something as basic as a charm or a piece of jewelry, talk in terms of personal benefits instead of just features. Instead of going on and on that the necklace is made out of white gold, tie that into the very human need to stand out from the crowd and feel like one matters.

Few people want to be just another face in the crowd. Most people want to feel special. Most people want to feel like there is only one of them.

Tie that while gold feature with the need for individuality and specialness. Maybe you can play up the fact that white gold is fairly rare. Perhaps you can play up the fact that this involves some sort of unique alloy. Whatever the case may be appeal to your prospective buyer's need for uniqueness. This is what I mean by tying personal benefits to product features.

Don't just list down the product features and expect the reader to figure it all out. You have to speak their language. You have to speak to their needs.

Hallmark #2

Present Social Proof

What if I told you that people are like sheep? I know it sounds harsh but it's true. People, at the end of the day, are more likely to engage in behavior when they are assured that other people have done it before them. You have to present some sort of social proof in your product descriptions.

You can mention that a lot of people have already bought this product and have great things to say. You can also import reviews or activate a special review section for each product on WooCommerce.

Whatever the case may be and regardless of how you do it, you must present social proof. You must put away any questions in the minds of your prospects that whatever you're selling is untried, and unproven. Nobody wants to feel like they're guinea pigs.

Hallmark #3

Write in a Direct and Personal Way

As much as possible, write in the second person. Use the word "you" a lot. People want to feel that you are speaking to them directly. In fact, if you do this right, you may be able to make them feel that you're speaking only to them.

Whatever the case may be when you get under their skin and you create an intimate bond between your text and the benefits it talks about and your customer, you increase your chances of making a sale.

Let me put it this way. If your perspective customer looks at your proud of description and is given the impression that you're speaking to that person directly, you're going to stand out. Why? Most of you competitors are just copying and pasting the manufacturer's product description. It's missing that special touch.

Do yourself a big favor. Go the extra mile and put in the time, effort and energy in writing direct and personal product descriptions. If you can't do this, because you don't have the time or the talent, hire a professional. It's that important.

Hallmark #4

Effective Product Descriptions Are Easy to Read

It's extremely important that you avoid the natural tendency to hide behind jargon. It's tempting to do this. It really is. If you feel that you don't really know what you're talking about or if you feel that you're dealing with some complicated topic, one of your first instincts is to just throw out complicated words out there.

These are so specialized that you think they would buy you credibility and authority. After all, most people don't talk that way. Most people don't even have an idea what these words mean. Your hope is the mere fact that you are using these means you are an expert or a credible authority at some level or other.

In other words, if you can't dazzle people with brilliance, you baffle them with BS. Well, that strategy doesn't work when it comes to product descriptions. It may work in college term papers or employee reviews, but they won't work when it comes to selling products.

Your descriptions must be easy to read. In fact, they must be so easy to read that people with only an eighth reading level can quickly get what you're trying to communicate. Other than that, you're going to lose people. Worse yet, you might even turn off people because it's obvious that you're just spouting out jargon or listing out specifications without a clue as to what they mean or the real benefits they bring to people's lives.

Hallmark #5

Highly Effective Product Descriptions Are Short or are Written to be Read Quickly

Let me tell you given the fact that more and more people are using mobile devices like smartphones and tablets to access the Internet, people's attention span is getting shorter is getting shorter and shorter. There are no two ways about this.

This is why you have to format your product descriptions in such a way that they can be easily scanned. Don't expect them to be read. Are you formatting certain words so they jump out and communicate value? Are your descriptions short enough as a whole?

Do you get to the point quickly?

It's okay to write a fairly involved product description but don't turn into a hassle for the reader. Maybe you can put subheadings. Perhaps you can bold certain words. Possibly, you can reduce certain things to bullet points.

Whatever the case may be when people read different sections of your product description, they must get the point quickly. If you write your product descriptions this way, you increase the likelihood that the reader will convert.

Otherwise, you may have a great product in your hands and you may be driving high-quality traffic to your website but you lose out at the end. At the very best, you settle for cents on the dollar; at worst, you're not converting at all. That's a tragedy, and a lot of the times, this is due to badly written product descriptions.

Chapter 9

Launch Your Store

Make no mistake if you're launching your store, you shouldn't do it without any advanced planning. In many cases, you only have one chance to make a good first impression. You don't want to launch your store with a lot of parts missing faulty product descriptions. That's like throwing a line out to the water when you're fishing and after you've forgotten to use bait.

It's a good idea to do a soft launch. This is a test launch. What you're basically doing is you're just notifying your friends and family members to check out your online store and try to break stuff. That's always fun. Tell people to check out your store, click on links and see what's going on.

The understanding is if they find anything wrong or badly formatted or missing, they should let you know. Also, you should have your staff for your freelancers check out your online store to spot problems.

This is crucial. You're not doing this because you have nothing else better to do. This is a very important part of your online store development process.

Since this is a soft launch, all feedback is going to go to tightening up the store. Maybe the graphics are off. Perhaps the product descriptions are not ready for prime time. Possibly, your pictures are not all that good. Focus not just on technical stuff but on qualitative issues as well.

Please don't get me wrong. This doesn't mean that your store launch must be absolutely perfect. Get that idea out of your head. There is no such thing as perfection.

There is such a thing as perfect enough. So, shoot for that because if you get the idea that you should launch when everything is completely perfect, you're going to take forever. Seriously. In many case, it just doesn't happen.

Do yourself a big favor. Identify a point where you can conclude that everything is perfect enough and that you should launch. In the meantime, make full use of this limited release to get all the information you need to whip your website into the best shape possible.

Full Launch

I know what you're thinking. You probably are under the impression that there is really not much difference between a soft launch and a full launch. You've already notified your friends and family for your soft launch. How different could a full launch be?

Well, it's actually quite different. If your mindset is that this is just a simple matter of a certain deadline passing, you're probably not going to do well with your dropshipping business. I know that sounds harsh, but it's the absolute truth.

You have to understand that the old idea of "build it and they will come" is a dead end. It really is. You can't just put up a website and somehow, some way, expect people to hear about it. It doesn't work that way.

Believe it or not, the real work begins once your website is up. Even after you have put in all the time, effort and energy needed to make sure that every link on your website works and your payment processing is smooth, once you get these things out of the way, that's just the beginning.

A lot of people cannot accept this. At the back of their head, they're thinking that making money online is supposed to be some sort of get rich quick scheme. Get those notions out of your head. This is real work. This is a real business.

Please understand that one definition of business is a set of activities that all involve solving problems. You get paid to solve problems. That's the essence of business. Either it's somebody else's problems or your own internal issues, you get paid when you solve those problems.

The precise opposite of this is to set up an enterprise and just sit back and expect things to fall into place. You're not solving problems that way. You're not delivering full value to your customers and to the system that you have built.

Again, once you have launched your website and you are sure that everything is good to go, that's when the real work begins.

You have to have a promotions to-do list ready when you launch. This is when you hit the ground running. Without this promo to-do list, you're basically taking shots in the dark. Worse yet, you're only taking action based on what feels good, feels right or feels inspired.

I don't know about you, but the last time I checked, people who are truly successful in anything continue to do what they're supposed to do regardless of how they're feeling. Maybe they woke up on the wrong side of the bed, maybe they're not really feeling all that inspired or imaginative a certain day, it doesn't matter. They just keep going. They are able to find the energy to put one foot in front of the other.

This has nothing to do with feelings, it has nothing to do with whether you think everything is going right, but it has everything to do with your ability to commit. This is the real deal. And unfortunately, a lot of would-be dropshipping millionaires blow it past this point.

They are able to put up amazing looking websites. I have to hand it to them. These online stores are extremely professional-looking. They even manage to put together an awesome graphical brand.

Unfortunately, there is a missing ingredient that ensures that all of these go up in smoke. That missing ingredient is promotions.

In Chapter 10, I'm going to walk you through a sample blueprint for the type of promotions you should run for your online store.

Let me warn you, a lot of people are under the impression that you're going to have to come out of the gate with both guns blazing and just put in hundreds of hours' worth of promotional work.

Well, you're more than welcome to do that, but here's the secret. It doesn't matter how much time and effort you put into promotions. What matters is consistency.

I've seen everything. I've seen people start their online store extremely idealistic. They would spend 160 hours in one week promoting their store. They start getting results, and guess what happens?

That's right. They stop whatever they were doing. They believe that they have paid their dues because they burned white hot for that one week. In their minds, this excuses them to coast for the rest of the remaining 51 weeks.

What do you think happened? That's right, their business did not go anywhere.

Consistency is crucial in this game. Even if you can only manage one hour to two hours of promotions per week, as long as you're focused, know what you're doing and are consistent, you will get results.

This reminds me of the classic story of The Tortoise and the Hare. The hare was all confident that he will blow away the tortoise because he's so fast. Sure enough, right out of the starting gate, the hare or rabbit pulled away from the tortoise. It was not even close.

In fact, the hare got so far ahead of the tortoise that he thought it was a good idea to sleep. After all, he had so much distance on the tortoise. Sure enough, the hare overslept and the tortoise won the race.

It didn't matter if the hare ran double time when he realized that he overslept. None of that mattered. What mattered is that the tortoise slowly but surely put one foot in front of the other. You should do the same. You just have to be honest with yourself.

If you can only devote two to three hours of promotions to your online store every month, then so be it. As long as you stick to that time budget and you use it wisely, you will get results.

Compare this to devoting those two to three hours to screwing around, checking your email, clicking on ads and messing around on Facebook. That's not research, nor is it marketing.

When you commit promotions time to your dropship business, it has to be focused. It has to involve pure implementation. You're not there to screw around, you're not there to research, you're there to execute. That's how you get ahead in this game.

Shortcut

Make no mistake, whether you're doing a test launch or a full launch, it can be hard on you. If you are a one-man band and you have a lot of things on your plate, chances are, your dropshipping business, as awesome as it may seem, will fall between the cracks.

It turns out that you have other more important things to think or worry about like your family, your day job, school, along with a long list of other concerns. This is too bad because the moment you allow yourself to get distracted, you won't be able to achieve the launch success that you have imagined.

The launch success, of course, is just simply making sure that everything works and your website is ready to generate sales. There's a shortcut to this. Hire virtual assistants from places like cognoplus.com.

I recommend Cognoplus because they list virtual assistants who would work a full 8-hour day for $30. That's a big deal because in the United States, the federal minimum wage is $60 per day plus required benefits and insurance costs (and possibly other employee benefits). If you were to factor in all your costs, your benefits and insurance and all that, you're going to be paying way more than $60 per person.

When you hire a freelance virtual assistant from Cognoplus, you get a college educated, dedicated, hardworking person who speaks English, to do whatever promotional work and site testing tasks you can assign. The quality of people you get through virtual assistant listing services like Cognoplus blows away hiring people off the street in the United States or Western Europe.

What can you assign these people? Well, for your soft launch, you can assign them link testing. Basically, they just check all the links on your website to make sure nothing's broken. They check all the photos; they check all the descriptions to make sure that they're all grammatically correct.

You can train them or tell them to load the text of your website into tools like copyscape.com to get rid of duplicate content. Duplicate content is bad news because it can kill the SEO of your website.

You can also ask them to read the materials to make sure that everything makes sense. You can even tell them to load every piece of text on your website into a grammar checker to make sure that your website is written in solid English.

After that, once you have fully launched, you can assign your virtual assistant low level promotional work. This is promo work that involves copying and pasting, getting lead information, that kind of thing.

Chapter 10

Conduct Consistent Full-Featured Promotions

As I've mentioned in a previous chapter, this is where the rubber meets the road. This is it. Your activities from this point on will either ensure your success or doom your venture to failure.

It is your choice. Seriously. Success is not something that happens to you. It's something that you create.

Understand that. Wrap your mind around that fact. There's no random chance here. There's no luck of the draw. This is it. It's something that you create.

How? Consistent full-featured promotions. That is your answer.

In this chapter, I'm going to spell out five ways you can promote your website for free or nearly free on the internet.

This doesn't mean that you should not sign up for paid advertising programs like Facebook ads or even Google ads. However, I suggest that you know enough of the ins and outs of organic marketing and fully test your website's ability to convert traffic into cash before you start paid advertising campaigns.

Issue a Press Release

A lot of people think that press releases don't work. A lot of people are under the impression that press releases don't do much good. Well, if they think that, it's because they don't know what they're doing.

A press release has to be written the right way so it can grab the right people's attention. Who are the "right people?" These are bloggers, news website editors, and commentators. That's the whole point of a press release. You're trying to grab media attention.

Now, they're not going to care one bit if your press release simply just hypes up your online store. So what? You're the one millionth dropship business opening its virtual doors this year. What's so noteworthy about that? How's that any different from the 999,999th dropship stores that opened before you?

The secret to press releases is to find trending news topics that relate in a very direct way to your niche. For example, if you are launching an online reputation SEO service, you can mention the rise of identity hijacking on the internet. This is when people make up all sorts of fake news regarding certain industry personalities.

You can hitch a ride on that trend because it is a very troubling trend. People do sit up and pay attention to that news because it's bad news. You can bet that bloggers, editorial writers as well as news reporters are concerned about this trend because it's a big deal.

In your press release you would say that this is a problem, and then you throw in some statistics that you found from other third party sources, and them massage in your service. What is it about your service that can help people recover from such attacks? What kind of service offerings do you present that would enable people to prevent this type of problem?

Do you see how this works? At the end of the day, your effective press releases are newsworthy.

Now, what makes this complicated and difficult is the fact that, by and large, business press releases are boring. They're so specific to their industry. They're so focused on promoting themselves. Nobody wants to read that stuff.

But if you find some sort of hook or angle that would connect whatever it is you're doing with a broad news trend that people are already talking about, you can get favorable news attention.

You benefit from press releases in three ways. First, you can get your press release copied and pasted in high quality blogs and news websites. This rarely happens, but when it does, it puts you in the spotlight. Your brand gets to attract many eyeballs. Also, this leads to people seeking you out for the next two benefits that I'm going to outline.

The second benefit are interviews. Usually, news reporters are not just going to copy and paste a press release when they're writing their story. Instead, they will contact resource persons who have very interesting stuff to share. They'll get a hold of you via email, you write whatever you want, and then they will incorporate your quotes and insight into their final piece. And usually, they would mention the name of your company or, better yet, link to your company.

The third way you can benefit from this is when news reporters actively want to do a story on your company as part of a larger story. This goes beyond an interview. Instead, they're doing a profile of your company either as an example or as some sort of centerpiece for a larger story that they are doing on a trending topic.

Once again, press releases are intended to draw the media's attention. All the benefits flowing from the press release, either direct traffic or high quality backlinks as well as industry credibility and authority, all turn on how newsworthy your press release is.

Start a Quora Campaign

I don't care what kind of product you're selling, there are bound to be questions regarding that product. If you can list down all these questions and you can answer them in a very professional way without resorting to hype and exaggeration, you have yourself a Quora campaign.

Basically, you would find existing questions on Quora and answer them in such a way that it draws attention to your online store. Now, there's a trick to this. I'm going to go into this in some length in the section below on "1-2 Punch Content Marketing."

Pardon the awkward term, but the 1-2 punch approach to content marketing works. It is able to deliver solid value to people who are actively looking for the kind of solutions your products solve.

A well-conducted Quora campaign is very selective in the questions that it answers. It also produces individualized answers. These answers are not self-promotional. Instead, they would use reference links that give people a broad overview of the problem.

Once they get on that page, they can then click through a more targeted list of solutions. From there, they can click through to your online store.

I know that there are a lot of steps involved, but as I will explain in the section on 1-2 punch content marketing, this actually increases your likelihood of attracting the right people and converting those individuals.

Create Social Media Accounts on All Platforms

If you are selling products that are heavy on pictures, you cannot dispense with your own Facebook page, Facebook group, Twitter, Pinterest and Instagram accounts. Ideally, you should also have a YouTube account if you have models or people who are actually engaging with the products you are selling.

It's important to create an official account on all these platforms so you can keep reinforcing whatever impression people have of your brand. This is crucial.

So if you have a certain design on your main store and blog, make sure those graphical branding elements are replicated throughout your network of social media accounts. Sure, these accounts would have different dimensions, they would have different texts, but generally speaking, they should look similar enough to each other that they keep reinforcing your brand.

Once you have set these up, don't stop. You're going to have to stock them with content that makes your brand more credible and authoritative.

Conduct a Content Curation Campaign on Social Media

This is crucial. You have to get content that establishes your authority, expertise and knowledgeability in your product niche.

Remember, for somebody to buy stuff from you, they must first trust you. That's very difficult. After all, you're dealing with perfect strangers. Thankfully, over the internet, this can be simplified.

Here's how it works. For somebody to trust you enough to buy stuff from you, they must first feel that they like whatever it is you are offering. For them to like your offerings, you have to give them the impression that you know enough about your industry and that you're giving them the right advice. They also have to be convinced, at some level or another, that they know enough about their problem for them to like whatever it is you're recommending.

Do you see how this works? So it starts with them feeling that they know enough, and then being led to liking a particular solution, and then getting enough information for them to trust the specific product that you are offering that fits the solution that they like.

Now, you may be thinking that this takes a long time. Well, for some people, that is absolutely correct. Some people take a long time to convince.

However, as I've mentioned in a previous chapter in this book, people no longer read on the internet. They scan. And believe it or not, thanks to mobile devices, trust formation has accelerated.

In other words, instead of taking days or hours to make a decision, people become so impatient and have such short attention spans that when presented with the right sequence of information, they can develop enough trust to take action on purchases.

This is why social media curated content is crucial. When you use a tool like Hootsuite or Buffer, you publish the very best content in your niche on different social media platforms.

You then target hashtags on those platforms to attract specific audiences. These audiences search for those hashtags, so you know that they are specifically looking for certain niches.

How do you know these hashtags? Very simple, reverse engineer your competitors' accounts.

For example, if you're selling baby shoes, look for baby shoe sellers on Facebook, Instagram and Twitter. On those platforms, they often use hashtags. List out all the hashtags that you dig up. Focus on the most common ones. Tie your curated content updates with these hashtags.

Using the tools that I mentioned earlier, you can rotate your hashtags. What's important is that you establish your credibility and authority with audiences from social media by presenting only the very best curated content.

Please understand that this content doesn't link to your online store. Instead, they go to somewhere else. But when people realize that your brand can be trusted regarding certain niche hashtags, they're more likely to keep coming back to you. This is what you want to achieve.

You're not looking at this as a short term game where you're basically just spamming hashtags in a desperate bid to get clicks to your online store. That's how many people play it, and they often fail. The better way to do this is to build a brand.

And if you've set up the right website with the right graphical branding as well as the right values targeting, when you offer high quality content in your niche, people are more likely to trust your brand.

Eventually, these people can become loyal, and that's when you should mix in your original content. This is content that solves people's problems and directs people to your online store and blog.

The good thing about social media curation is that it can be simplified on two fronts. First, when it comes to content selection, you can use a tool like BuzzSumo to find out the hottest pieces of content in your niche. Instead of fooling around Twitter trying to figure out what's hot in your niche, you can easily use that tool to pull the shared content on social media that is hot in your niche.

I can't even begin to tell you how awesome this is because it saves so much of your time and effort. It really does. Why? When you run a search on Buzzsumo, you can see the social signals of those content.

You're not just taking random pieces of content that people like to share. No. You would see whether something gets retweeted a lot. You can see whether a piece of content gets a lot of shares on Facebook.

When people do this, it means that the piece of content is, more likely than not, valuable. This means this is high quality content. You can then safely curate it and expect the people you attract to find value in the content you're sharing.

This keeps them coming back. In fact, it may keep them coming back to the extent that they see your original stuff too, and they click through to your store. Do you see how this works?

You cannot build a curation campaign on garbage. The stuff that you're sharing is going to have a direct impact on the brand that you're trying to build. This is why you have to be very selective regarding the quality of the content you are sharing on your official social media accounts.

You can't just pick random pieces of content because they have certain keywords that are relevant to your niche, but it turns out that nobody reads these articles. Either they're written badly, they're boring, or they just have low quality information. Whatever the case may be, you end up damaging your brand when you curate garbage content.

Focus on building your brand curating only the very best. BuzzSumo is a great tool for helping you quickly figure out which piece of content is truly viral in your niche.

Again, the strategy here is very simple. Build a following curating the very best content in your niche as determined by social media signals. Once you have built up your following, start rotating in some of your original content so you can get direct traffic to your site.

Also, AliDropship has a sister product called Social Rabbit, you can find them with a lower price if you buy AliDropship Plugin, it can help you automate your eCom Business with Social Media and their auto-posting features. You should try it.

Build a Mailing List

It's extremely important that you build a mailing list. I suggest that when you set up your online store, people would have to sign up for your mailing list before they place an order. This is crucial.

Why? When you have people on your list, you get to take many bites at the apple. That's really the simplest way to explain it.

What do I mean by that? Well, I have some depressing news to tell you. The vast majority of people who visit your website will never ever come back again. In fact, most of them will instantly forget about your website the moment they exit. That's the harsh reality.

Now, what makes this depressing is that you obviously put in the time, effort and energy to draw those people in in the first place. It really is quite sad that they are simply just too eager to forget all about you and move on to the next website they're browsing. They didn't buy anything, so they will completely forget your site.

If you have a mailing list, you would have a way of contacting people who have either bought stuff from your website or who have signed on to your mailing list because of some sort of freebie you're giving away.

It's extremely important to build a mailing list because you can recycle much of the traffic your website would attract in the course of its life.

Now, you may think that after you launch that your website doesn't really get much traffic. Well, it just seems that way. Sure, you may get less than 20 visitors per day, but that's still 600 people per month.

Now, can you imagine if you had a mailing list and you successfully bring back 20% of that number? That's 120 people.

When you send an update and 120 people show up to your site, you are enjoying a traffic volume that's six times your average. When you increase your visitor rate by that much, there's a good chance that you can convert some of those people into sales.

Also, when you send updates through your mailing list, don't be surprised if your list members share these updates. When you send really interesting content that they like, they might share it on social media or they might even forward the email.

Make no mistake, if you want to build a solid brand and you want to convert at a higher level, you have to have a mailing list.

1-2 Punch Content Marketing

As I've mentioned in a previous section, you have to adopt a 1-2 punch content marketing strategy for you to make money with free traffic.

What makes content marketing complicated is the fact that most people are not going to buy something the moment they read an article. When was the last time you bought something just because you read an article? I'm willing to bet that those times are few and far between.

You are absolutely normal. Most people do not buy something just because they read a piece of content. You have to create a layering system to drive people from one piece of content to another piece of content so as to increase their level of trust. This way, you use content as a filter.

Here's how it works. You set up Page One. Page One is a consumer guide.

For example, if you're selling baby shoes, you would publish content like "Top 10 Qualities of the Kind of Baby Shoe Your Kid Will Love." These are consumer guides that project your expertise and knowledge.

When people read this, they basically get an appreciation of how knowledgeable you are regarding your niche. In other words, they're asking themselves, "Does this person know about my problem?" And, more importantly, "Does this person know enough to solve my problem?"

This is how you filter people based on your knowledge. And you also give them the impression that they know enough about the problem to like a particular solution. The point of this type of page is to get people to feel like they know enough about their problem and that you are the expert educating them.

This page is not flat nor is it passive. This is crucial. You cannot create a first level page in 1-2 punch content marketing that is flat. In other words, people come in and you say, "Okay, this is your problem, these are the solutions. Have a good day." That's worthless. You're not serving yourself when you do that.

You're in this game to make money. You're doing this not because you have nothing else better to do, but you want to make money. So have to write or get your writer to write a Page One piece of content that establishes credibility, maps out different options, and gets people excited about the particular type of solution category your products fall under.

This is where Page Two comes in. If you have well-written Page One content, they act as filters for people who are more likely to eventually buy. People who are just curious or are not ready to buy get the information, think you're a genius, and move on. On the other hand, people who are ready to make a move on their problem read your content, see your credibility, and click on a link because you've convinced them of the particular type of solution you are offering.

Again, you're not selling your specific product. You're just selling a type of solution.

So this Page One links to Page Two. On Page Two, that's when you have a specific product review. These are actual reviews of products found on your website or similar products competing with products found on your site.

The person clicking through would see these products lined up against each other. They will get information on the pros and cons of these products. When they click through, they then end up on your product description page.

Technically, there are really three levels here. Because on Page One, you get people to know solutions to their problems. On Page Two you get them to like a specific solution. And on Page Three, you get them to trust your solution.

But I'm only mentioning Page One and Page Two because these are the pages that you have to write for marketing purposes. These can vary depending on what you're promoting.

The third page must already exist. The third page, of course, is your product description.

Please read the portion of this book that talks about product descriptions. I want you to wrap your mind around that information because this is crucial. This really is your conversion page.

If you drop the ball on Page Three, all that hard work you did for Page One and Page Two would be for nothing. So make sure you invest in the very best product descriptions. These are the pages that would turn traffic into cash.

1-2 punch content marketing is really just a variation of the old online sales funnel model. When you take a funnel, you would notice that it is very broad at the top. This is the mouth of the funnel, and then it gets narrower and narrower. And then at the bottom is where the fluid comes out. It is very narrow.

By the same token, your Page One is very broad because it's forced to get general traffic from your social media accounts, your press release and other sources, and then start filtering that traffic narrower and narrower until your Page Three converts a relatively small percentage of that broad traffic into actual sales.

The Secret

The secret to succeeding with 1-2 punch content marketing is actually pretty straightforward. You have to pour traffic on Page One.

Now, do not misinterpret me. I'm not saying that you should spam Page One. I'm not saying that you should just buy junk traffic and pour it on Page One. That's not going to work.

Instead, focus on featuring only the very best niche-specific authoritative content on your social media accounts, articles, blog posts, and all other marketing platforms. This has to be solid material. And then from these link to Page One consumer guide type of content.

This is how you filter traffic so as to increase the level of trust and credibility that traffic has in your brand. You're not just pouring a huge amount of traffic to your Page One page. Most people don't have a clue what you're talking about. Most of them won't care.

Also, if you use unscrupulous traffic sources, a lot of them would feel like you're tricking them. Not exactly the mindset of somebody likely to buy, right?

So it's really important to use the content that you are using to build credibility on social media platforms, press releases and other traffic channels as your first filter. People who would read that stuff are interested in your niche.

Now, the point of those materials is to filter people based on how interested they are. So if they're interested enough, they go to your Page One content. And if these people are interested enough in a specific type of solution, they then drill down to Page Two. And from there, you are more likely to convert those people into actual buyers.

This is the secret. Pour traffic on Page One. How? Create lots of content.

The good news here is that it doesn't have to be your content. It can be curated content. Meaning, as long as you're providing a link to the third party source of that high quality content, you create a win-win solution.

It's not like you just copied and pasted their content. If you did that, you'd be stealing from them. That is illegal as well as unethical.

However, if you are supplying a link to the content and you're also supplying your own link, you create a win-win solution. You use high quality, proven content to attract qualified traffic, which can then go to your 1-2 punch content layout.

Conclusion

Making money online using your own dropship website has become so easy and cheap. Back in the bad old days, setting up an online store was a very expensive proposition. It had a high barrier of entry.

You had to buy inventory, you had to lease a warehouse, you had to hire people, it was a mess. It is no surprise that the vast majority of people who tried traditional online retailing simply failed.

Now, thanks to dropshipping, you can set up your own online store empire at a fraction of the cost. However, there is so much hype regarding this type of business that it's very easy for you to get distracted and adopt strategies that lead to failure.

What I've laid out in this book is based on my own hard won personal experience. You may be thinking to yourself, "Why did he cover these topics and not others?" Well, the explanation to that is quite simple. I only wrote about practices and techniques that I know work.

How do I know? Well, they worked for me.

So do yourself a big favor, look at this framework and apply it to your set of circumstances. Plan based on your resources and your timeline. Once you have set forth a plan, execute it. That's right, do it.

A lot of people get stuck in analysis paralysis. They think that as long as they can get the right piece of data, they will not fail. So what they do is they keep researching dropshipping. They buy book after book, and never get around to putting up an actual business.

People who get stuck in analysis paralysis are simply just giving themselves excuses for not starting. Don't do that. It's much better to take action now and then fine tune later rather than expecting the perfect plan and never getting around to taking action.

As the old saying goes, life is what happens when you're making other plans. Too many people get caught up in the planning stage.

They think that everything has to be perfect. Everything has to line up. Everything has to be just right.

Well, when they do that, they're giving into their fear because they're really so deathly afraid of failing that they give themselves excuse after excuse not to start.

My final advice to you is traffic. Please understand that just because you've built a good looking website, it doesn't mean that you will be successful. This business, believe it or not, doesn't turn on looks. Instead, it turns on traffic.

You have to get traffic to your site. Without traffic, you're not going to make any money. Last time I checked, Google's search robot doesn't have a credit card. You know who does? Actual visitors.

So master the art of the 1-2 punch content marketing. Plug that into your social media publishing schedule, and you should be good to go.

The keys to success here are consistency and attention to detail. These go hand in hand.

If you need any additional help, visit my website https://6figuresclub.com where I offer Video Training Tutorial, Done For You & Coaching Programs, also you can know my Story, we might have more in common than you think.

I wish you nothing, but the greatest dropshipping success.

6 FIGURES CLUB®

[22]

---

22. https://6figuresclub.com

DROPSHIPPING *for* HEROES

ANDRES & LOLY ZAMRIVER

Did you love *Dropshipping for Heroes*? Then you should read *Blogging For Cash - First Edition*[23] by Andres Zamriver!

24

How would you like to learn how to get paid quite a decent amount of moneydoing things that you love?

This sounds pretty awesome, right? Wouldn't it be great to get compensated handsomely for doing things that you otherwise would gladly do for absolutely free?This is exactly the kind of lifestyle many successful bloggers enjoy.

Simply put, they get paid to write or collection information about stuff they're passionate about. You get paid to have fun. You get paid to live life to the fullest.

Blogging for cash also enables you to turn your spare time into cash.

---

23. https://books2read.com/u/b5OVKk

24. https://books2read.com/u/b5OVKk

Best of all, blogging produces passive income.Unlike a job where you have to show up and work for eight -hour blocks of time,or else you don't get paid, if you blog for a living you can go away on a long tripand your blog will continue to make money even though you're not activelyworking on it.

You only publish once and the income for that post continues to roll in. Sure, it may be a tiny income stream for each post, but if you have hundreds of posts on your blog, this can easily add up to quite a substantial and a very welcome amount of cash.

This is the power of passive income. It totally liberates you from how most otherpeople earn their money.

Active income essentially forces you to live like a chicken.

Do you know how a chicken makes its living?

It has to scratch into the ground for it to get its food. If it doesn't scratch, it doesn't eat.

This is why a job is spelled J-O-B. This is an acronym for **Just Over Broke**.You're essentially just chasing your tail and trying to keep one step ahead ofinflation.

Unless you break into the ranks of upper management or you become a CEO, working with other people means you have to chase after promotions or tryto get substantial pay raises.

Otherwise, you're essentially going to be stuck trying to keep your head above water for a long, long time until you retire.

When you create a powerful passive income system through blogging, on theother hand, you create a system that enables you to earn money regardless of how much you work.

You can be taking a long extended vacation with your family and you would still be earning.

This book teaches you how to blog for cash the right way. Just like with anythingelse in life, there's a right way and a wrong way to do this. Unfortunately, mostpeople choose to blog the wrong way.

This is why they fail. There are certainonline income secrets involved in blogging for cash the right way. I 'll show you HOW. Enjoy

Also by Andres Zamriver

Blogging For Cash - First Edition
Dropshipping for Heroes

Watch for more at https://6figuresclub.com.

Also by Loly Zamriver

Dropshipping for Heroes

Watch for more at https://6figuresclub.com.

About the Author

Andres Zamriver, M.A., is passionate Entrepreneur and eCommerce Consultant along with his lovely wife Loly who holds a B.A. in International Business.

Together, they established an online business which they successfully operate in the comfort of their own home (Zamriver Corporation).

To date, Andres has authored an array of books and training courses on all things eCommerce, blogging, online marketing & branding.

His primary mission is creating positive change in people's lives through the power of internet-based entrepreneurship.

During his spare time, you can find him spending quality time with their two beautiful children (Angel & Vicky).

He also enjoys watching soccer games and relaxing at the beach.

Read more at https://6figuresclub.com.

www.ingramcontent.com/pod-product-compliance
Ingram Content Group UK Ltd.
Pitfield, Milton Keynes, MK11 3LW, UK
UKHW022006190726
13853UKWH00004B/1766

9 798201 046118